"She'll be right...
Yeah, Nah"

A Kiwi girl's guide to depression –
for your whānau, the bros and your squad.

Katie McQuaid

A catalogue record for this book is available from the National Library of New Zealand.

ISBN 978-0-473-69015-1

Book design & layout by Vanessa Edridge

Printed in New Zealand by www.yourbooks.co.nz

This book has been printed using sustainably managed stock.

Disclaimer

The views, thoughts and suggestions in this book are purely my own and have been formed through my own experiences. If you need immediate help, please seek advice from a professional such as a GP, a trained counsellor, or a mental health practitioner.

Where to get help:

1737, Need to talk?
Free call or text 1737
to talk to a trained counsellor.

Anxiety New Zealand
0800 ANXIETY
(0800 269 4389)

Depression.org.nz
0800 111 757 or text 4202

Gumbootfriday.org.nz
Free counselling for anyone
in New Zealand who is
25 years of age or under.

Lifeline
0800 543 354

**Mental Health
Foundation**
09 623 4812

Rural Support Trust
0800 787 254

Samaritans
0800 726 666

Suicide Crisis Helpline
0508 828 865
(0508 TAUTOKO)

Yellow Brick Road
0800 732 825

0800 What's Up
0800 942 8787
(for 5 to 18-year-olds)
whatsup.co.nz
Phone counselling and online
chat available.

Youthline
0800 376 633,
free text 234,
email talk@youthline.co.nz, or
online chat and other support
options at Youthline.co.nz

In a life-threatening situation, call 111.

To all my people,
beyond blessed for your love and support.
I wouldn't be here without you.

For anyone who needs to hear it –
you are so loved.

x

Introduction

Depression is a big word.

It can mean many different things to many different people. There are books, podcasts, studies and literature out there around depression and how to deal with it if YOU'RE the one going through it.

But what if it's a loved one that's struggling?

I've suffered from depression and during those dark times I found that my friends and family often didn't know what to do, or how to cope, or how they could best support me - and back then, there didn't seem to be a simple way of explaining it to them.

*"I have been trying to process what this means for me and how to move forward. I guess it feels like admitting that I have depression means **I'm not as strong as I once thought I was**. And at the same time, maybe it means that I will be strong eventually. Part of me feels like it's a weakness but when I think about other people suffering through this as well it's definitely not about being weak. It's the opposite. A big part of me wants to scream from the rooftops that I'm struggling but at the same time, I want to curl up in a ball, hide under the duvet and not see anyone at all. But I know that I can get through this and maybe one day, help to break the stigma surrounding mental illness."*

*"Today was particularly hard but I can't pinpoint exactly why - it just was. I'm guessing that some days just suck for absolutely no reason. The feelings envelop me and **I feel the need to escape**, to somewhere where no-one knows me, there are no stresses, no worry about work, no friends or anything. I can just be alone. But at the same time, **being alone is what scares me the most**. I know that in order for me to get better, I need to be truly content on my own and love myself. Somewhere along the way, I lost track of how to do that."*

After a car ride home from a touch tournament one Saturday evening, a teammate gave me the much-needed push in the right direction to make a start on this book. He talked about how he was wanting to write a book and I mentioned that for quite some time, I had been wanting to write one as well.

"Go on, do it. Five lines per day. When you get home tonight, write your five lines and send them through." This was the motivation I needed. So, I started writing this book in the hopes of sharing my experience with others but I also wanted to provide tangible advice along with simple steps that could be taken for those closest to a loved one living with depression.

I can't stress this enough but everyone's experience with this silent illness is different - so take what you can from this.

It might be snippets; it might be one paragraph that resonates or it might be a whole chapter. However these words reach you, this is my story and my perspective. But if it manages to help one other person by reading it, that is all the gratification I need.

Contents

Don't let anyone dull your sparkle

1

Katie's story

To be truly vulnerable means searching the deepest parts of our souls and finding the essence of who we truly are - the good, the bad and the ugly. Vulnerability for me means being okay with it all.

This is my story of how I came to realise I was suffering from depression - the despair I felt, the triggers that lead me to that place and my slow but steady steps towards living with wellness.

I grew up on the Kāpiti Coast in a small town called Paraparaumu. It was a good upbringing and I was a pretty happy kid. If I think back long and hard, I could say I've probably been dealing with depression for a good nine or ten years now, possibly even longer.

Depression. This mental illness has got me.

It's taken me a long time to truly accept it for what it is but I finally feel okay enough in myself to want to share my story. Because that's what this is about. Talking about it. Normalising it. Helping our young people (actually, helping **anyone**) to feel like they're not alone. It's important that we speak up, lead by example and don't shy away from what's important, from what matters.

I liked going to school when I was young as I was fairly smart and liked to learn but this also opened me up to some bullying. It wasn't outrageous but more so the usual comments that kids can sometimes say. I don't remember ever not wanting to go to school so I don't believe anything in those early years impacted me greatly. When I got to high school though, it was a different ball game. I think that the transition from primary school to high school can be quite unsettling for a lot of young people and I definitely wasn't the exception. I was short (still am), a bit awkward and lacked confidence in myself in many different situations.

Although I knew I was intelligent, I didn't see this as a strength of mine and chose to downplay what I knew so that I could be more "normal".

The typical teenage approach to trying to fit in.

I started to experience regular feelings of not being good enough and started seeking different avenues to find my place. Sport provided me with an amazing outlet and as it turns out, I wasn't half bad. I wasn't the greatest but I could hold my own and worked hard to compete despite my height disadvantage. I made some wonderful friends who, to this day, are still important people in my life. Sport taught me hard work, problem solving, discipline, drive, teamwork, communication, strategizing, sportsmanship, resilience and many more life skills that have helped shape me into who I am today.

Over the teenage years, I started to form my own identity. As I mentioned, I lacked confidence in myself.

I cared a lot about what people thought of me and I felt pressure to act and behave a certain way.

So, I strived to be the best I could be in every aspect of my life, whether that was achieving excellences at school, or pushing myself in sport or trying to be the most social and fun friend I could be. Those expectations came about for a number of reasons: I wanted to make my parents proud, I was motivated to do well academically and sport was (and still is) my passion, my outlet, my way of expressing myself. When I'd do well, the part of my brain linked with positive endorphins would tell me how good it felt and simply put, I wanted more.

But these unrealistic expectations were exactly that - unrealistic. And when I didn't achieve those things, I felt like I had not only let myself down but that I'd let my parents down as well.

From an early age, I recognised that my parents wanted the best for me and my brother. They instilled values in us such as working hard to get what you wanted. You had to be grateful for what you had and that things didn't just arrive on a silver platter. They read to us, played with us, helped us with our homework, set firm boundaries and pushed us to reach our goals. I think that definitely motivated me to want to please them but I also think I started to set myself unrealistic expectations in the hopes of impressing them. Particularly my father. Yes, I wanted to do well for myself too but when I didn't, or when it didn't match my brother's successes, I felt like I wasn't good enough and that I had let them down. My Dad's relationship with my brother has often been a bone of contention as I've felt like he was the favourite child. We joke about it to this day and I've made peace with the fact that their relationship is different to my own relationship with Dad. But as a teenage girl who wanted to feel just as important but never quite got there, this became hard to deal with.

I know my Dad loves me and I love him. Over the years, I've learnt a lot more about his story and his experiences which have contributed to a greater understanding of how he parented us. But those teenage years were tough and the arguments with Dad became a trigger for me. I was starting to form my own identity and beliefs about how I viewed the world and this would often not align with my Dad's views.

When my brother left to join the Navy after finishing high school, things got progressively worse for me. It was clearly a change in dynamic and I'll admit that I was pushing boundaries where I could. But I wasn't a bad kid and I didn't think his controlling behaviour was helping things. My parents would often have arguments as well and I would find myself caught in the middle - mainly defending Mum. It never got physical but the verbal disagreements were enough. Children understand more than you might think and what I took away from that over the years has strongly impacted my views on love and relationships (more about that later).

I can't speak for my parents and what their relationship was like for them - I can only speak to what it was like for me as their child. To have thoughts that your parents remained together just for the kids was a tough pill to swallow. But I genuinely believed that when I was a teenager. They didn't seem to get along all that well, there was minimal affection shown when I was around and the way they spoke to each other didn't portray a happy relationship. I said at the start of this paragraph that I know my Dad loves me. Knowing this and hearing this though - are two completely different things. My Mum always says "I love you" or "love you" as we end phone calls, when I go home, or at night before bed. Maybe that's a Mum thing. I'm sure Dad said it to us regularly as kids. But from my memory, I could probably only count on one hand the number of times that my Dad has verbalised it to me over the years.

So, there's always been this need/desire to make him proud or to impress him to get that gratification and that verbal reassurance that I am good enough.

These feelings continued over the years when I left home and went to university. I felt the need to prove myself by getting good grades and getting the degree. I met a lovely guy and we dated for three and a half years - but the relationship was far from perfect. We were young and we both made some mistakes.

And at the age of 21, I made one of the only decisions in my life that I've ever truly regretted.

I think we all make choices along the way and when we stuff up, we learn from them. But this one was an epic fail. I was unfaithful and for someone who has lived their life up until this point with honesty and loyalty, the devastation was huge. The carnage that followed ate me up for years. I was humiliated, embarrassed and ashamed. And it took me a very long time to make peace with what I had done. Everyone makes mistakes and I know that I never intended to hurt him. I was young and dumb. I vowed to learn from my mistake and made changes so that it wouldn't happen again.

I was screaming out for that love to make me feel worthy but couldn't recognise at the time that he wasn't able to give me what I was so desperately seeking. What I was seeking I could only truly find within myself.

Over the years that I tried to be perfect, I failed to take notice of the most important aspect of life: recognising that I'm only human. Nobody is perfect. Yet after a few years of constantly seeking perfection, the mind allows you to think that it's attainable. Let me tell you, it bloody isn't! That's not to say that I don't still want to live my best life, it's just that now I know my best *is* good enough and I'm happy with that.

A wise colleague once said "your 80% is someone else's 100% so stop trying to be perfect and know that your 80% is good enough".

Words of affirmation have always been my love language so I guess it makes sense that I was in constant need for those words of reassurance from Dad. When they didn't come, I would get upset and frustrated because I found it so easy to communicate my emotions and couldn't understand why he couldn't. But I'm learning that I'm highly in-tune with how I feel and can effectively verbalise this while many people struggle expressing themselves. It's unrealistic for me to place those expectations on others and as I mentioned before, this has impacted considerably on my own relationships over the years and the types of men that I've dated.

I've often sought partners who I've hoped can show me love but who, upon reflection, have generally tended to be emotionally unavailable. I dive straight in hoping to prove myself, get attached quickly and then I'm devastated when it doesn't work out because I've tried so hard.

But love shouldn't be hard right?

Recognising the patterns is a starting place but putting in the hard work to change these patterns continues to be a work in progress.

2013 was the year I lost my Grandad. Grandad had been diagnosed in the early 2000's with prostate cancer but refused treatment because my Nana (who passed away prior to me being born) had gone through chemotherapy for her cancer and he hated what the treatment had done to her. Science and medical advances had come a long way since then but Grandad had it clear in his mind that treatment wasn't an option. He lived alone, visiting Nana every Sunday at the cemetery but was always quite content in his lifestyle.

He'd met his one true love and nobody was ever going to replace her.

Fast-forward ten years and Grandad was walking out to the mailbox to collect his newspaper. He takes a tumble and when he comes to, continues on to the mailbox and THEN decides to call the ambulance. He's rushed to hospital in New Plymouth (a one-hour drive from Hawera) and the doctors tell us the cancer has spread to his lungs, his liver and his bones. The prognosis wasn't good but Grandad being the champ that he was, pushed on for another three years.

In the year prior to him passing away, the cancer really got to him. Because he was living alone at the time and all of our family were spread over New Zealand and Canada, he had nurses coming daily to help around the house (which for someone as independent and proud as Grandad must have been quite humbling). But for the rest of us, it eased our minds knowing that he had people checking up on him. At this stage, the cancer was too far along to have surgery so the doctors recommended radiation as a treatment. Grandad came down to Palmerston North and I remember visiting him with my Mum and Aunty in the accommodation across the road from the hospital. Grandad was clearly in pain but putting on a brave face for us.

Mum and Aunty Jo had to head off so I accompanied Grandad in the courtesy van to the hospital for his radiation treatment. We're driving along and once we arrive there shortly after, Grandad steps out of the van himself instead of waiting for some help. I'll never forget the intense grimace of pain that shot across his face as his feet hit the pavement (the cancer was most prominent in his hips and pelvis bones). Thankfully, an orderly arrived right away with a wheelchair and he was able to rest before being taken inside. I kissed him, wished him luck and told him that I would see him again soon. I jumped back into the van with the driver, who took one look at me and said "Honey, it's okay - let it all out" so I sobbed and sobbed and sobbed in front of this complete stranger. Body-wracking sobs.

Yet it was one of the most cathartic and healing five-minute car rides I've ever had - to simply be able to express your innermost pain and to not feel so alone in that. The lady driving the van was a godsend and to this day, I'm extremely grateful for her kindness, understanding and compassion.

Grandad passed away a few months after that - I think he was too weak and the radiation too strong. He'd planned his funeral to the nth degree with the plot beside Nana ready and waiting - he wasn't a showy man so only wanted family at the funeral. The funeral was tough, with Mum and her four siblings trying to make arrangements with all of their emotions flowing.

Unfortunately, words were said that weekend that couldn't be taken back and arguments ensued with a particular rift between one sibling and the rest of them. It was messy and it was hurtful. At a time like that when five children have lost their remaining parent, I can only imagine the grief they must have been experiencing, all the while trying to arrange things, look after their own families and do the best they could. But it was one hell of a time.

And then on the car ride home, Dad proceeded to fill me in on how our family had been left out of family holiday trips over the years and that Grandad stopped visiting us as much as the other grandkids.

I was perplexed and hurt - at not only the grief of losing him but also finding out that another relative had been unable to provide the love I so desperately wanted.

I had so many questions for Grandad yet I was so gutted that now I couldn't ask him. It all seemed so unfair. I remember arriving home the night of the funeral and just sitting there. I sat for a good hour, feeling numb. Feeling pain and grief and loss. Just a sense of utter devastation for what I thought my childhood had been to facing some confronting truths. Some were sad, some were painful but I guess that's a part of growing up. You're faced with hard truths and sometimes they're going to hurt.

I called my best friend Tara that night and she could sense it had been a traumatic time. She asked what happened and I couldn't even muster the courage to go through it again as the emotions were so raw. Two other friends passed away that year and I really started to question the meaning of life and death. I've never been religious so I don't believe in the afterlife but I also don't think it just ends there. A good friend shared a book on spirituality with me that really resonated and helped me to process all of the grief and loss I was experiencing.

In 2014, I was lucky enough to travel to America and worked at a summer camp over there. These were some of the happiest times of my life - I fondly remember watching the fireworks over the Disneyland castle and thinking to myself that this was what life was about. The small things. I was truly independent over there in the sense that I had to rely on myself living so far away from home. I also lived in Whistler for seven months after camp and engaged in the typical lifestyle that many young travellers do.

There were lots of alcohol-fuelled nights and the hangovers to match. And there were also times where I struggled being in that lifestyle. I remember a few nights out where I had to leave the nightclub after feeling a panic attack coming on.

Alcohol is another trigger for me and has been for a number of years. It allowed me to numb the feelings of emptiness I was experiencing and instead replace those with a sense of escape.

Throughout my university days, I was drinking and partying two-to-three times a week which I considered normal and in New Zealand at the time, it probably was. The drinking continued over the years, peaking again while overseas. And then once returning home, the pattern continued. I think I found a particular comfort in being able to let loose and not feel the pressure to behave or live a certain way. It was unhealthy and I know that when I'm feeling down or having a depressive episode, I can't touch a drop.

When I arrived back home from overseas, I was tired. Not your usual tired though. I felt depleted, my energy levels were low and even though I had just had this amazing experience, things were weighing on my mind.

Looking back now:

- my view of my parents' strained relationship,
- my relationship with my Dad,
- my own failed relationship and indiscretion,
- loss,
- grief; and
- alcohol

all compounded for a pretty toxic situation. I hadn't dealt with any of it properly so the next year was a bit of a blur until I found myself in a fog.

I was working as a Health and Physical Education teacher at the time, had recently accepted a role as a pastoral Dean for the next year and seniors were just about to go on exam leave so my workload had ramped up considerably. I found myself struggling to go to work each day.

I literally woke up every morning and would go through all the excuses I could find so that I wouldn't have to go.

But I did. I dragged myself in each day even though inside I was screaming. I was calling, texting or visiting one of my good friend's Mum - Jen (pretty much a second Mum to me) every other day during that time as I had no idea what was going on. There were feelings of despair, of not being able to cope and this constant need to get away from it all. I genuinely didn't know what was happening. I was putting on a performance for everyone else - family, friends, workmates, as it was easier than being honest with them about how much I was struggling. On top of that, I didn't want to let anyone down or to be seen in a certain light. I didn't want to be a burden.

A common tell-tale sign at the beginning of my depressive episodes is extreme tiredness but it's not always easy to spot depression.

I'm thankful I had a friend who knew me better than I knew myself and recognised the changes. She had also experienced something similar with her brother and was able to correlate what was happening. But it wasn't straightforward or as simple as me thinking "crap, I feel bad, I'm going to go see the counsellor/doctor and get diagnosed." Jen had to convince me and cajole me almost on a daily basis to come to those conclusions because if I hadn't been willing, there would be no way I would have gone to the doctor.

I didn't want to admit I had a problem. Especially one with so much stigma.

I wonder how many other people suffer quietly with mental illness and don't speak up because of that stigma. I knew something was wrong. I knew I wasn't myself and hadn't been for a long time. And I also knew that if I looked deep within and was truly honest with myself, I had some serious unresolved issues that had been simmering away at me for a while. I don't think I ever thought I had depression until Jen suggested it. I remember visiting her one of those days and I was mentally drained. She took one look at me and said "Shorty, your eyes are glazed" and I said "yep, I'm beat" and she just knew. That same conversation happened multiple times over a period of two to three months where she would notice my eyes were glazed and that I was struggling - big time.

When I was initially diagnosed, it was a relief because I finally had some understanding about why I had been feeling the way that I had been feeling. Numb.

Foggy. Joyless. Wanting to see the sun but never being able to get rid of the clouds.

I think that's been the most accurate description to truly encapsulate what I had been feeling. But then the realisation sunk in that I had a problem, and then the fact that I had to deal with that problem. It was overwhelming, it was scary and it felt like everything had changed. I mean, I thought I had my shit together - I'd been travelling and living overseas (having a blast I might add), I'd come back to a fantastic career, supportive friends and family, and I had a passion and zest for life. Yet if I was truly honest with myself, other feelings had been sitting just beneath the surface for a number of years, without me realising or actually having the courage to see them for what they were. This was confronting in ways that I couldn't have thought possible but having a reflective, soul-searching nature, I finally was able to make a decision to tackle things head on and seek help to get better.

Because at the end of the day, who else is going to fight for your life if you're not?

Once I finally relented and visited the GP, coming to terms with the diagnosis and what that meant for me was the next part of the battle. Because even though I now had answers for what was happening, knowing didn't necessarily provide me with the strategies or tools I needed to work through it. That took time. And it was a lengthy process - one which I continue to this day and will continue working on in future. It's easy to sit here now and say that I've got a toolkit of things I can use or strategies I can put in place to help myself but it wasn't always that way and it wasn't always that easy to use those tools.

Take exercise for example. I know that exercising is one of my tools - it can be as simple as going for a walk or a short run, it could be a home workout or a high intensity game of netball. So, I know that I can do those things to help make me feel better. But actually putting it in practice in the midst of a depressive episode took far more courage and strength than I've given myself credit for. Some days (a lot of the days actually) I didn't even want to get out of bed. I knew I had to and I knew that to keep functioning I needed to do those little tasks. But then to exercise as well on top of those little tasks - some days it was too much.

Too much to even put my shoes on, tie my laces and walk out the front door.

I guess the point I'm trying to make is that even though I knew exercise was going to be good for me, the actual reality of forcing myself to engage with that tool was physically and mentally challenging. It was f**king hard. To have that kind of battle on a daily basis wears you down to the point that the menial tasks become the focus and the tools that you know can work take a backseat.

I started writing in a journal a month after I started seeing a counsellor, to try and sort through my thoughts and make sense of my feelings on a day-to-day basis. Reading back through these still brings up emotions today but I'm confident in my ability to sit with these emotions and recognise them for what they are: sadness, hurt, and pain. But that's **okay**. Those are completely normal feelings that everyone experiences in life. Yet we live in a society that tells us constantly to be happy, to be outgoing, to be confident. Social media provides a somewhat glorified platform for people to share only a portion of their lives, the "filtered" portion, and in doing so, disguises the times when we struggle. I'm definitely guilty of this myself as I'm sure many of you are but it's time that we address the harm this can cause and the pressure it places on people to be "perfect" all the time, whether that be self-inflicted or otherwise.

It's okay to not be okay.

It's okay to feel like crap when you've had a shitty day at work or when you lose a netball game or when you have an argument with your Mum or Dad. What's not okay though is feeling like you're alone in that, or that you have no-one to turn to.

Along with the counselling, writing really helped me as an outlet so that I could transcribe my feelings. Here's an insight into what I was experiencing in those first few months:

"There are some days or some moments when everything just feels right. I got home from netball trials, had a shower and while sitting in bed, I felt this wave of calm come over me. And it's been a while since I've genuinely felt that way. It's nice. I can't explain the reason why I feel good, just as much as I can't explain the reasons why I might feel bad - I just do. But I'm learning to appreciate these moments of calm and truly let myself embrace them. To be fully in the moment. I think sometimes it's so easy to get caught up in all the bullshit, in work, in stress. It can be so easy to lose perspective so when these moments of calm and clarity come, I want to grab it with both hands and not let go."

"It's 11.32pm on a Sunday night and the feelings of not being worthy/feeling shit about myself are all consuming at the moment. I can't seem to switch my brain off or change my thoughts to positivity.

It's funny because I can almost feel myself slipping down into those emotions but at the same time, having absolutely no control over stopping them.

I'm starting to recognise the warning signs - wanting to be alone, overthinking things."

"This journey is proving to be a whole lot tougher than I first imagined. The fact that I can wake up feeling relatively normal and then hit rock bottom by the end of the day still surprises me. And the opposite as well, feeling crap in the morning and still feeling crap by night. My thoughts are never-ending and I guess a part of me questions whether this diagnosis is leading my mind to these places and whether I would still feel this way if I didn't get an answer. It can be so confusing because even though there are parts of my life that I feel in control with, there's still quite a lot that I don't. The feelings of irritability that come out of nowhere. And yet at other times, I feel great."

It probably took me all of 2017 to start working towards using my tools effectively. It was a hard slog and it was every day. I relied heavily on my counsellor during that time along with Jen - as she had been there throughout my teenage years, knew me wholeheartedly and was able to provide level-headed guidance based on that knowledge. This balanced quite well with my counsellor who didn't know me like that and who offered an unbiased and professional lens.

I think I want to highlight here that it can be easy to become dependent on your counsellor. Their job is to prompt you to come to your own conclusions about your situation and then devise strategies with you to be able to manage things on your own. Yet it can be so easy to continually seek that advice and support even though you might have the skills within to do it on your own. I did become dependent - probably both on Jen and my counsellor.

I felt like my whole life as I had known it had been thrown upside down and I was clinging to the proverbial life-raft.

I knew that I actually had the skills I needed to get through this though. I was just petrified that I might not get out the other side. To have to face a mental illness head on when you thought your life was going down a different track was hugely unsettling and was a whole new reality. When I started opening up to my family and friends, the love and support they provided and continue to show me to this day reinforces how much I'm cared about and loved. And that is the most important thing.

think
positive

talk
positive

feel
positive

2

So, what can you do?

Once I bit the bullet and decided to open up to people, I received an extremely positive response. I think unfortunately there is still a lot of stigma attached to the word depression but I think it's getting better. There's more knowledge and openness out there yet I believe New Zealand still has a long way to go.

At the time, the emotion that was overwhelmingly at the front of my mind was shame.

I didn't want to admit that I had a problem, that I had this "thing" that I had to deal with. And I most definitely did not want it to define me. I see myself as successful, motivated and driven. So, to have to admit to myself that I wasn't okay was a challenge in itself. It's hard at the best of times to admit weakness or to have to ask for help but I'm so glad I did.

A lot of people private-messaged me after my blog to say how they felt - that they were inspired or that they were proud of me. A few people also messaged asking questions and wanting to know more about what they could do to help. Or they had someone close to them going through something similar.

What I've maintained through my experience is that depression is different for everyone. So, there's no one real answer or quick fix.

But there are some things that my people did or said that really made a difference. And there are some things that I wish they had said or done at the time which would have made a difference. But they didn't know. It was never their fault – but a lot of my frustrations that manifested within me came from feeling misunderstood. Feeling like I was alone. Even though I know I wasn't; it was a mindfuck all the same (excuse my language). Because if you haven't been through it or experienced those feelings of helplessness, how are you to understand or be able to share a similar perspective?

A common theme that came through in some of those questions was that the family member or friend just didn't know what to do. Or how to help. Or how to be there for their loved one. My best friend mentioned that over the years, she often felt this way. She didn't know if she was doing enough or the right thing to help me through those times. It struck me that maybe there wasn't easily accessible information out there, specific to New Zealand.

Sadly, our suicide statistics in New Zealand are some of the worst in the world and it boggles me that our Kiwi attitude of "she'll be right" still exists.

Don't get me wrong, I believe we are opening our eyes more to what depression (and other mental illnesses) actually means but I think we still have a long way to go. It's being able to challenge the status quo and the typical Kiwi mindset of pushing through when times get tough. Yes - let's build resilience but let's also recognise that sometimes it isn't that simple.

Education is a fantastic place for some of these discussions to start. Through my role as a Health and Physical Education teacher, I've been blessed with the opportunity to (hopefully) inspire and enrich my student's lives - to be able to have meaningful conversations in a safe and supportive learning environment. To be able to use my personal knowledge of depression and what it can do to a person has been extremely beneficial in being able to reach out to our young people. Part of that education process is allowing people to voice their thoughts and opinions; and to feel like they've been heard.

If your child comes to you and says they'd like to talk and it's on a topic that makes you uncomfortable, all you need to do is listen.

It sounds like simple advice and yet we so often get caught up in figuring out our response that we don't actually listen to what is being said. When you're in a room of 28 fifteen-year-old girls, trust me - you gotta listen! And sometimes, more often than not, it's listening to what isn't being said:

- Noticing the change in someone's expression.
- Picking up on a change from their usual routine (such as sleeping patterns or their eating habits).

My advice here: don't be afraid to *ask the question*. Even if you don't have the answers, your loved one will hopefully feel an immense sense of relief that someone has noticed enough and has cared to ask. Then actually listen to the response. Sometimes we feel the pressure to not ask the question because we don't have the answer. But it's okay to not have all the answers. When someone asks how you're doing or notices a change and actually has the balls to ask you about it - that means something. It meant something to me.

Being there can mean the world to someone who is facing a constant dark cloud and a feeling of nothingness.

I'll stress it again - you don't have to have the answers but you've got to ask the question. It might be as simple as "I've noticed that you don't seem like yourself lately, is everything okay?" Or it could be along the lines of "I care about you - can you tell me what's going on?"

For me, it was a sense of relief to feel like I could offload some of the pain. I know that I'm a very reflective person and find being able to talk through things beneficial but that wasn't always the case. I used to put on a brave face and pretend like everything was okay because I felt pressure to behave in a certain way. Most of the pressure came from my own perception that I was supposed to be happy all the time. My life was good in the sense that I have family and friends who care about me, a solid job, a roof over my head, so what was the problem? Once I was able to open up properly and start to make sense of my feelings, it was then that I could start learning about my triggers and actually make progress towards being well.

Don't be afraid to ask the question even if you're scared of the answer you might get. We're all doing the best that we can and for your loved one, it could be just the opening that they need.

Just because
my path is
different,
doesn't mean
I'm lost

3

Knowing the triggers

In the couple of years and months prior to my diagnosis, there were a handful of situations that I recognise now were clearly red flags. Alcohol has been involved in a few of these and that's been another battle in terms of controlling the temptation to just let loose and knowing that when I'm feeling low, drinking just isn't a good idea. One particular situation was a night out in town with a couple of friends, and the anxiety overtook me.

I felt like I couldn't breathe, like everyone was looking at me. I felt like I needed to escape.

I had a full-blown panic attack, to the extent that my friend and her flatmate took me to A&E at 3am because they couldn't calm me down. I remember thinking "they probably think I'm just a drunken mess, why did she drink so much?" but even though I was under the influence, the anxiety was real. The thoughts going through my mind were negative and then the influence of alcohol meant that they spiralled. By 5am I'd sobered up enough to regulate my breathing so we went back home and went to sleep without seeing the doctor.

I woke up feeling embarrassed and ashamed and I remember thinking to myself "how can I get out of here quick enough to avoid the questions?" I felt terrible for my friend and her flatmate, which only led to more guilt and self-loathing.

There have been at least three other situations where I've been in social settings with alcohol involved, where those feelings of anxiety have hit me so hard that I've needed to leave then and there. Without telling anyone and without explanation. Obviously not the smartest of moves but dealing with the anxiety has also been a steep learning curve. Putting my friends in that type of situation seemed very unfair and I know that I'm blessed to still have those people in my life because it would have been easy for them to not understand, especially when I didn't understand myself.

For about a four- or five-month period, I couldn't shake the feeling of this cloud sitting over me. Work was a struggle, I found myself finding reasons to not hang out with my friends when usually I'd be jumping at the chance to be social.

I'd lost interest in doing the things that mattered to me the most.

I remember crying at night in bed for about a week for absolutely no reason, then berating myself almost immediately afterwards for being pathetic. One day I found the number for a counsellor, rang and hung up, then convinced myself I was fine. There was a lot of denial during that time as I hadn't really experienced those feelings over an extended period of time. I genuinely don't think I ever considered that I had depression since it was such a foreign concept to me. But the feelings were real and so was the problem.

Did I have suicidal thoughts in those months? The easiest answer to that is kind of. I mean, there were times that I thought about having a car accident, a simple slip of the wheel.

But I never dreamed of following through and I hope that I never will.

Depression makes you believe that you're not good enough and that no one will miss you. Even when that's an outright lie.

It makes you believe that the pain will go away. That the heartache will stop. That you're doing people a favour. There's still this common misconception out there that if we talk about suicide, that it will encourage people to do it. I'm sorry but that's the dumbest goddamn thing I've ever heard.

Having these conversations about how we feel when we're at our lowest is the key in preventing these tragedies. Not being afraid to be open and honest with your loved ones. Being real about feeling shit and acknowledging that it's okay to feel that way. Asking someone how they're doing and actually listening to the answer.

When one of my brother's friends committed suicide during high school, my Dad and I had an honest and open conversation, which didn't happen all that often. It was one of those moments that I'll always remember. We both felt it was such a waste and tried to make sense of something that even adults struggle to comprehend. He said to me that "tomorrow will always be there if you let it. The sun will always rise." That has always stuck with me and in my lowest moments, it's the knowledge that the sun will always rise that has got me through.

Tomorrow has the chance to provide a better day.

I didn't recognise the signs for a long time but when it all clicked into place, it made so much sense and it struck me that I hadn't found help sooner. But that's the thing with mental illness, you don't really know you've got a problem because you're so consumed with the feelings that it just becomes a weird sort of normal. We place so much pressure on ourselves all the time and for what? Whichever way you look at it, imperfections are what makes us all human. And that's exactly what we are: human.

Looking back, I recognise another big trigger for me was when my Grandad passed away in 2013. Even though I was initially diagnosed by my GP at the beginning of 2017, I believe I've been living with this illness under the surface for numerous years.

Some forms of depression are situational - which means that under particular circumstances where extreme levels of stress are present, a depressive episode can be triggered.

When Grandad died and the funeral ensued, the level of emotions that I experienced during that weekend were, simply put, horrendous. It took me a long time to process those emotions. Not only losing my Grandad but the hard truths that came along with it. I think that was one of my first serious depressive episodes and it lasted a while. But it makes sense, right? Life and death situations create heightened levels of stress so of course there was going to be some fallout. I just didn't expect it to last for as long as it did or for it to have such a profound impact.

I lost two other friends that same year so by September I was really questioning it all. What was the purpose? I know that death is a natural part of the cycle but when cancer and accidents happen, taking those you love too soon it's really shitty. There are no other words - just shitty. Writing this has brought up those emotions again but I'm okay to sit with them now and see them for what they are. Sadness combined with fondness but also a sense of peace that they're no longer in pain.

I recognise that that was a time in my life where I struggled big time and really didn't know what to do. But we pick ourselves back up and continue on, day by day if we have to.

Something tangible that you can do with or for your loved one is to sit with them and write down their triggers.

Actually write them down in a list. This way, it can clarify for them what things/tasks/objects they need to avoid or to be mindful of and helps both them AND you to recognise when they might be in a potentially negative situation.

Throughout my journey, I've been blessed with an amazing support person (amongst many) - the mother of one of my good friends. Jen talked me through this process on the phone one day and as confronting as it was, it helped me to specifically identify the self-destructive behaviours that I was exhibiting. There was no hiding. And as painful as it was at the time to open myself up to scrutiny, it was probably the best exercise I've done in relation to living with depression.

For me, my triggers include:

- arguments/disagreements with Dad,
- drinking alcohol,
- being super stressed at work, and
- negative self-talk.

And as I mentioned above, losing loved ones. You're probably thinking "of course" but for someone with depression, going through the grief process is that much harder because our minds are wired differently. I'm not saying that we feel it harder but the easiest way to explain it is that the emotions are vivid and the thought processes become entangled. What has worked effectively for me though is being able to notice the trigger early and put in place my tools to prevent me from spiralling downwards. In doing so, I'm more easily able to self-regulate and (hopefully) prevent another depressive episode.

In relation to situational depression or anxiety, it's about recognising any small changes in personality or moods or even a change in their routine. If you're noticing your loved one experiencing higher levels of stress: whether that be school or work-related, relationship issues or the illness/death of another loved one, please please please ask those questions:

- **Are you okay?**

- **What can I do to help?**

- **I'm happy to sit here and listen - I don't even have to say anything.**

- **What do you need?**

- **I hear you.**

- **I'm here for you.**

They sound like simple questions and statements but in those times, it can be so easy to forget or to get caught up in everything that we need to actually go back to the basics. Human connection is a part of our nature and the comfort that can be felt by hearing those words can never be underestimated.

Identifying your triggers:

When you're feeling low, what makes things worse?

**What are some things/situations that bring
on these feelings?**

My triggers are:

One of the
most beautiful qualities of
true friendship
is to understand
and to
be understood

4

Just being there

It sounds so straightforward right? Just being there.

Just be there for your partner.

Just be there for your friend.

Just be there for your son/daughter.

But as I mentioned earlier, one of the most common responses I received from friends and family members was "it just doesn't feel like it's enough". I think for someone who has never had feelings of depression or anxiety, it might be hard to fathom or even begin to comprehend the weight that lays on the shoulders of your loved one.

The brain has rewired itself to make that person think differently and consequently affects every aspect of their life: their self-esteem and self-worth, their ability to complete daily tasks, their relationships, their work life and levels of motivation.

What's important to remember here is that for everyone, their thoughts manifest *differently*.

That means that for one person who is living with depression, they might still have positive self-esteem and be able to function relatively normally at work but they might cry themselves to sleep at night as they just can't seem to find the motivation or sense of purpose within themselves. For someone else, it might mean that they can't get out of bed on a daily basis as the thought of simply facing the world is all too much. For another person, depression could be that every aspect of their life is planned and organised to the extreme because if it's not, they'll have a meltdown and lash out at anyone close to them.

I know it's hard to imagine something if you haven't experienced it yourself. You can empathise but it's different to living it. For example, I have no idea what it would feel like to live with cancer or to be fired from my job. Yes, I've had loved ones go through cancer and loved ones pass away from the disease. I've also known people who have been let go from their jobs. I can empathise with people who have lived those things but as I haven't personally experienced them, I really wouldn't have a full understanding of what they have been through.

The old saying "don't judge someone until you can walk a mile in their shoes" or something like that - it's true in all senses of the saying. And very true when it comes to depression.

Because it's a mental illness and not physically present, it can be easy to shrug off or be difficult to imagine what it might be like for someone. We can all imagine having a broken arm or some sort of physical pain because we've all been physically hurt before (I'd be very impressed if someone had never been physically injured!!) but not everyone has experienced mental pain. Or more accurately the constant feeling of mental pain. A day-to-day feeling that never seems to relent. No matter what you try or how successful you are or how good your family is.

Depression doesn't judge - it can affect anyone.

So, although spending time trying to put yourself in the shoes of a loved one with depression may be helpful to understand what they are going through, it is not the be all and end all. Because understanding what someone else is feeling is not always straightforward. Part of understanding involves just being there, asking the right questions, and listening. This could be enough to help that person open up and/or take positive steps towards getting better.

Throughout my time as a teacher, I've had many times where I've been able to be there for my students. It's both a blessing and a curse to be in education - a blessing that you can positively influence the younger generation and a curse that you have the potential to negatively influence the younger generation! But I've always loved and had a passion for building relationships with my students. That feeling of being able to relate to them on a whole other level really can make a difference.

Sadly, for a lot of teenagers, school is their safe place. It breaks my heart that in a country like New Zealand where we are well and truly developed and have systems in place to support those most at risk, an alarmingly high number of kids are going hungry, don't have enough money to buy basic supplies and live in a society where domestic violence is still very prevalent. Add the mental health issues on top of all that and we really need to question whether we're doing enough to help our young people.

One situation I recall when I was able to be there for someone was when I was teaching on the Kāpiti Coast and I noticed a change in one of my students. I had taught him in Year 9 for PE and Health and he was such a cool, spunky kid.

He even made me a little origami bird at the beginning of the year - just because.

He was into sport, very active and seemed confident around his peers. Making friends didn't seem to be an issue for him. It wasn't until Year 10 that I picked up on a few changes in his demeanour. I was teaching him three days a week so I was able to recognise these changes over a period of time. He was moody on some days, would put his headphones on during class and when I called him on it, I'd basically get an ignoring response. Or he'd only get back on task once I had walked away. Now for a Year 10 boy you might be thinking that's normal behaviour (and trust me, for a lot of them it is!) but for this student it wasn't. He was usually so respectful and polite, and generally had such a bubbly personality that it was concerning.

At this point, I think I'd been diagnosed a year or so prior so everything was fresh and new to me and I was still trying to figure out how to live with this thing. But I knew something wasn't right. I had a Health session with his class for the last spell of the day and his moodiness was ever present. There was a lack of response and a general sense of gloom so I kept him behind after class. I knew his Mum through netball and that he lived close by so he wasn't going to miss his bus or not be able to get home. I was nervous about bringing this up with him but trusted my instincts enough and believed that my responsibility as his teacher was to ask the question. So, I did.

I asked: "I've noticed that over these past few weeks, your mood has changed quite a bit. Do you feel comfortable talking to me about it?"

He nodded and it was the opening that he had needed. I asked a few more open-ended questions such as "What's been going on for you?" "Tell me about how you're feeling?" and then it was a lot of listening. It was very sad to see his pain and to hear about how he woke up each day not feeling great and that he was struggling to get out of the rut he was in.

I offered suggestions and strategies that he could use as a starting point (based on my own experience) - things like ensuring he had a good night's sleep, writing down three things he was grateful for each day. I also asked if I could let his Mum know that we had spoken about this. That's the other aspect of teaching that becomes tricky. In this sense, I wasn't concerned that he was a risk to himself (but if the situation didn't change, he might be) and I didn't want to break his trust.

I made it very clear to him that if I believed he was at risk, I would need to pass it on to the guidance counsellor.

But thankfully he was open to me discussing it with Mum. It meant that I could involve another person in supporting him and I knew she would do whatever she could to help. I also linked him in with Kāpiti Youth Support, a local non-profit organisation that has close ties to the community and the college itself. He was assigned a mentor and from what I recall, he started to attend some counselling sessions.

His Mum approached me a couple of months later while we were at the pub (small town...) and said how much she appreciated what I had done. She mentioned that he was working on things day by day and that their family had put other support systems in place. I was thrilled - there's no greater feeling than knowing that you've helped another human being. Especially when we all know what the most ultimate consequence can be.

Just being there can be ENOUGH.

Some of us think
holding on makes us strong,
but sometimes
it is letting go.

5

Feeling like a burden

As I've mentioned previously, my family and friends would often ask how I was feeling once I'd opened up with them about what I was going through. This was great because it meant I knew that they cared. That they cared enough to ask and genuinely hear the response.

However, the feelings that I was experiencing were often all mixed up and too hard to explain - a big jumble of nothing and everything all at once.

So, to try and put that into words for someone who feels normal most of the time seemed like a mammoth task. When you're in a constant state of numbness or feeling like a cloud is blocking your happy emotions, this can be hard for someone that's not living with depression to understand. Yes, we all have our bad days and our sad days. That's part of human life. But to feel like there's no light at the end of the tunnel can be all consuming, overwhelming and for some people too much to deal with. Sometimes the natural response to that is to self-isolate.

I know in my weakest moments that I want nothing more than to run away or to hide from the people around me. I struggle to want to communicate or have in-depth conversations. Work seems like an insurmountable challenge. Back when I was teaching, having to face 25 students, five sessions a day and act like everything was okay was just too much to bear.

I just couldn't face having to explain myself to another person because I thought that I was sounding like a broken record.

We've all got our own busy lives and I never wanted to be a burden to anyone. So those feelings would come in waves and my body's natural response to that was to hide. Not talk to anyone. You're a burden Katie, no-one wants to hear your problems AGAIN. You don't even have anything to be sad about. What's wrong with you?

The mind games had begun.

The trigger to negative self-talk.

A depressive episode wouldn't be far away...

At the beginning of 2021, I quit my job and relocated up north. I'd been having a terrible time at work for over six months due to a couple of work colleagues and their poor behaviour, so I decided that my wellbeing was my priority and that I wouldn't put up with the situation any longer. I made the move to Hamilton so I could push myself out of my comfort zone by trying something completely different.

I didn't have a job lined up or a place to live at that time but I figured what the hell, let's give this a go.

This was scary in so many ways as I was leaving the comfort of a familiar place and strong support networks to a whole new unknown. Particularly with the uncertainty of it all. Now if I had a dollar for every person that asked "why Hamilton?!" I'd be $72 richer! It's close to everywhere, the house prices were relatively affordable (well, cheaper than Wellington) and the tropical climate of minimal wind really appealed to me. I've since become acclimatised to the fog - it literally can sit there ALL day. Because there's no wind - how ironic. Anyway, I picked Hamilton, packed my bags and all of my belongings into a rental truck and drove 8 hours to my new home.

And then the reality of the move started to sink in.

I had quit my teaching job, moved to a new city, changed career and all of a sudden was faced with this new lifestyle. I knew that it would be a period of adjustment. Yes - I'd made that choice but going through those waves and just being able to sit with those feelings of uncertainty - that was tough. And when you live with depression, it only adds another layer of complexity as there's the risk of the situation triggering another episode.

I knew in my heart that I could cope as I had moved overseas and lived away from home previously. But I also knew that my mindset was the key to being able to adjust successfully. I managed to sit with those feelings in the first month or so - and then my car got broken into. That sucked. And then I had to decide whether to interview for the permanent role of the job I was currently doing. I didn't know what I wanted (I still don't) but I knew that having job security was important to me. And then my car broke down (after it being broken into only a few weeks prior) so I paid $500 for that to get fixed, only for it to then fail on its WOF. Then the heat-pump broke. Then I broke. I found myself driving to an appointment at one of my schools, trying to hold it together but failing miserably as the tears were streaming down my face. I was able to give myself a quick pep talk and pull myself together before the meeting. But only just.

It was at that moment that I realised the combination of all these things (mostly inconveniences) had triggered a downward spiral. I'd been feeling it brewing for the past couple of weeks and was trying to use my self-care tools as best as I could. Unfortunately, they didn't work and I found myself in a particularly lowish low.

I was mad at the world, mad at myself for moving away from all of my support systems and frustrated because things weren't going my way.

I couldn't seem to kick that mood. I was grumpy, irritable and was waking up each day feeling super anxious and wishing I could just avoid everything. It wasn't until a friend reminded me that sometimes your battery can be empty and you need time to recharge it before kicking back into gear. Those words were simple enough to allow myself a breather and recognise that I didn't need to have all the answers. Even though I was feeling out of my depth, I was still Katie. Even though things were feeling out of my control, there were some things that I could control. Like what I gave my energy to. The importance of exercise. The little things I could do and achieve to feel successful - like cooking dinner or cleaning the house.

Upon reflection, feeling like a burden throughout this situation limited me from reaching out for help sooner.

I think that I recognised my symptoms a lot faster than I had in the past so that was something, yet it was so easy to fall back into the familiar pattern. The negative thought processes returned and I quickly slid downhill into believing that I wasn't worthy of help and my friends and family would be tired of hearing about it. These thoughts prevented me from using the tools I had acquired over the years to actually be able to help myself and unfortunately it has been a common occurrence to feel this way especially when I'm struggling.

What I'm learning about myself throughout this process is that reassurance can really go a long way.

Hearing that I'm not a burden then following up on those words with action can really make a difference.

What I mean by this is give your loved one a call or a visit in the next day or so. And then check in again. Consistency is key. In my case, I need to believe and feel that you're free from judgement, you genuinely give a shit about me and want the best for me. Reassurance can show your loved one that they are not alone, that you have the ability to recognise what they're going through is tough at the moment and that you'll be there for them regardless.

This relates back to the earlier chapter of just being there. I know that when I'm feeling like a burden, the last thing I need is to be alone even though every inch of me is screaming to be isolated. My mind is telling me that people are avoiding me or that I'm being annoying but this is where I get in my head and make myself feel worse.

What you could do for your loved one at that moment is be there and stay by their side.

Give them a hug.

Hold their hand.

Sit with them and tell them that it will all be okay.

Sometimes we just need that reminder because at the darkest of moments, we're petrified that it won't be.

I may not be able to
solve all of your problems,
but I promise
you won't have to
face them alone

6

Teenagers

Oh, the blissful time of adolescence. The time when we start to discover our true identity in all our awkward and unique ways. I'm sure we can all remember our teenage years - for some of us this happens to be a lot more recent than for others. But I think it's safe to say that we know how life-changing this period of time is in our lives.

Being a teenager can be tough.

I've seen it first-hand where many of our young people are dealing with situations so complex that it's a wonder how they are actually functioning. For a lot of our rangatahi, school is their safe place and yet it can also bring uncertainty, pressure and additional stresses to their already complicated lives. This isn't to say that all teenagers experience angst and have trouble dealing with their day to day lives - but with the explosion of social media and the ability to remain connected 24-7, a number of issues have come about that many of us could not have foreseen.

When I was a teenager, cell-phones were just coming onto the market and the classic Nokia 2280 blue brick of a phone was all the rage. We played Snake and sent text messages with character limits because if you sent more than that you got charged extra. But I still talked with friends on the home phone and looked forward to going around to their houses to hang out (if Mum and Dad let me).

It was a simpler life with all the usual pressures of trying to fit in whilst not embarrassing yourself. Boys and crushes were a focus of course but sport took up the majority of my time. I'm thankful that a lot of my school friends who I remain in touch with today are friends who I grew up with playing sports. That shared passion of exercise, a team environment and working towards a common goal was a key motivator in keeping me on track. I still firmly believe that sport provides a prime opportunity for teenagers to gain a sense of belonging and the opportunity to develop their life skills such as problem solving, resilience, teamwork, communication, conflict resolution and much more.

However, technology and social media have a lot to answer for. The impacts of social media on a teenagers' wellbeing can have a potentially disastrous effect.

With the rise of assaults being video recorded and shared virtually; online bullying is at an all-time high and there is a pressure to conform to a non-realistic image of perfection - it's no wonder a lot of our young people are struggling.

But we can help, and a very basic part of that process is simply to understand that their experiences are VERY different to what we have experienced. A particular example of this relates to the male genitalia. I don't know about you but receiving my first nude picture (more commonly referred to as a "dick pic") via a dating app at the age of 29 (no, I did NOT ask for it) was somewhat disconcerting and for lack of a better word, yuck.

I'm a grown woman with a fair amount of dating experience but this; this was a whole new ball game - pun intended.

I did not ask for it.

I did not find it appealing.

I did not want to get in my car, drive over to his place and jump his bones - and the thought that he thought that I would is so far from reality that it makes me cringe.

What concerns me even more is that I have heard from a number of my students that this is deemed normal. That for them to receive a "dick pic" is just something that happens. Since when did a teenager have to deal with that? I believe it's like someone walking up to them in the park, opening their trench coat and flashing them. The only difference is that that person would hopefully be arrested for indecent exposure towards a minor.

The online world can be a scary place. So, discussions around keeping themselves safe are more important than ever.

Technology is rapidly changing and it can seem like a tricky subject to broach. But parents - you NEED to be having these conversations. It is important to keep in the front of your minds that the world we are living in now is very different to what it used to be, even just twenty years ago.

Being open to having these conversations can make a world of difference and can supplement what the education system is trying to keep up with and provide. A village raises a child and all people involved can make a difference. Especially parents.

Here are some helpful questions:

- What sites do you like to visit online?

- Can you tell me about some of the apps you like to use?

- Why do you like that app? What appeals to you?

- Have you ever felt pressure online?

- Are you friends with people online that you don't know?

- Do you feel safe online?

- Have you ever been bullied online?

- What kind of images do you post of yourself?

- Do you feel like that's a true version of yourself?

I think it's important to not be judgemental here.

You may not like the outcomes or the answers but at least you have prompted your child to open up and engage with you about where they're at.

You're essentially seeking a positive relationship and an open and honest conversation to encourage sharing. Sharing could lead to answers that you may have been seeking earlier but haven't necessarily known how to get to.

There is also a certain challenge in being able to recognise when a teenager is truly experiencing mental health issues versus just going through the trials and tribulations of everyday life.

I think from my perspective, it's about recognising the small changes and not being afraid to ask the questions even if you don't have the answers.

As a parent, you know your child inside out and sometimes probably know them better than they know themselves. Yet when the teenage years begin and the hormones start flowing, there can be this invisible barrier that prevents those open and honest conversations. This isn't always the case though as I know many young people who have wonderful relationships with their parents and can openly discuss any issues that they may be experiencing. But there are also teenagers who feel like you don't understand them or the pain that they're experiencing on a day-to-day basis.

Just because they're a teenager doesn't mean that what they feel isn't valid or true. As I've said earlier in this chapter, the pressures that our young people face these days actually blow my mind. All of the usual teenage things like the need to get that top grade for their schoolwork, the desire to fit in, or the other family responsibilities and expectations placed upon them. These are coupled with the constant barrage of social media content and messaging leading to the inability to actually "switch off" and take a break.

Letting our kids know that it's not the end of the world if they don't pass an exam is a step in the right direction.

Or if they don't make the sports team. Or if there is a photo of them posted online that they believe is somewhat unappealing. It just doesn't matter. Being able to refocus their thoughts on what's important and that failing is a part of our lives. What makes our character is our resilience and the ability to try again. If you don't get that top grade at school, what could you do better next time? Did you ask your teacher for feedback? Did you read the standard and what was expected properly?

Could you ask for more help? If you didn't make the sports team, what can you do to improve? Did you ask for feedback on your performance? Are you actually willing to put in the time to improve? If not, maybe it was a blessing in disguise that you didn't make the team.

The key message here - it's okay that you failed. Just make sure you keep trying.

Being able to take a step back from the situation and pragmatically reflect on where you're at can help to simplify your next steps. I've kept that in mind on many occasions when having these discussions with teenagers. Isolating the issue - what's actually causing them stress? Then asking what they can control. And in many of these discussions, the realisation that they can control certain aspects and not others, helps them to let those other things go.

We can't control other people's actions nor can we expect from them the same level of behaviour that we would demonstrate. The world just doesn't work that way. As soon as we're able to take that perspective on board and focus on what we *can* control, the levels of stress and frustration should also decrease.

As an adult, we have life experience that has taught us many things but I'd hazard a guess that we all know what the important things are: the people and relationships in our lives and being content in who we are. Our identity forms the beliefs and values we hold dear and informs the way we choose to live our lives. Therefore, being able to help our teenagers to keep focussed on what is important and not to sweat the small stuff can hopefully help them form their own identity and choose to live a life that makes them happy.

There is
always time
for a
cup of tea

7

A cup of tea

This short chapter is about being truly in the moment and enjoying the little things in life. I've read John Kirwan's book "All Blacks Don't Cry" a few times now and what stuck with me from that is how he helped himself to really focus on one moment at a time, particularly when he was feeling really low. It might not seem like much but the smallest act of drinking a cup of tea can have many positive effects for your loved one if they are struggling. Please note: the type of hot beverage here is irrelevant - I just don't drink coffee!

When I've been experiencing a depressive episode, the ability to look after myself and my basic needs seems to be so much harder than usual.

The smallest of tasks such as showering, deciding what to wear for the day or what to have for breakfast can feel like a massive challenge. This is because my thought processes are overwhelmingly negative and focussed on either what has happened in the past or what might happen in the future. This is why being able to be truly in the moment matters so much when a loved one is in that state. A simple cup of tea can be just the task to bring the focus back to that particular moment.

You might be questioning why this can be effective but it literally comes down to being able to focus on that moment in time.

And only that moment. Nothing else.

Depending on where your loved one is at, getting them to make the cup of tea can be a small accomplishment. It means that they have achieved a basic task and can feel proud of themselves for ticking something off their list. It may not have been on their list to start with but the act of completing something can reassure them that they are useful. That they do have the ability to look after themselves. On the other hand, if your loved one is incapable of doing anything, it's okay for you to make a cup of tea and sit there with them while they drink it.

The warmth of the liquid as it trickles down your throat, holding the cup between your hands while slowing your breathing down and the freedom that accompanies the moment - these are all the things that can refocus the mind. For me, the cup of tea is about allowing myself the time to be present and to not think about anything else BUT the cup of tea.

I used to always wonder why Nanas' and the older generations would offer a cup of tea in times of stress but now I truly get it. I understand.

They must have known that on some deeper level the ability to sip a warm drink actually forced the person to slow their breathing right down and to relax somewhat.

It didn't make the problem go away but it was a break in time that allowed the person a chance to step back from the weight that was currently on their shoulders. It provided an opportunity to reflect on the situation and to address their emotions on the matter. Life is busy these days - so having that time can be crucial.

Make that cup of tea.

Take the time out of your day.

Who knows; it might be the most important five minutes you'll ever take.

difficult roads
often lead to
beautiful destinations

8

Medication, counselling and exercise

Counselling has been my absolute saviour whilst living with depression. I'm not sure if you can tell from reading this book but talking, self-reflecting and discussing where I'm at comes quite naturally to me. I like having the ability to share my thoughts with another unbiased human and this continues to help me process the way my brain is working. For a lot of people, talking about their feelings and emotions may not come as easily and the thought of sharing their innermost feelings with a complete stranger could scare them off the idea of counselling completely.

But I keep coming back to the recurring theme of this book - that people need to talk. Have those conversations.

Encourage loved ones who may be struggling to push themselves out of their comfort zone so that someone can help them. No-one will know or understand how they feel unless they have the courage to talk.

Being a support person for your loved one can be the key to getting them help. As I mentioned above, just the thought of sharing your feelings with someone else could be a dealbreaker for some - so offering to go along with them for the first appointment is a great starting point. You could drive them there and just sit in the car or the waiting room; or you could even go in with them if that is something they'd like.

It's important that they know that you are there for them in what is likely to be an extremely vulnerable moment.

If they are struggling to book the initial appointment, this is a small task that you could also take on. My advice here is to explore what options you have available so that you can find the best fit. If your family member or friend doesn't feel a connection with the counsellor/psychologist the first time around, find someone else. I cannot stress this enough. The connection that you have in that space is of the utmost importance as this is where the professional support really plays a vital part. The trust needs to be there. If they don't feel safe for whatever reason, they need to listen to that and find another person.

Keep searching until they find someone that they do feel safe with.

I know that counsellors and psychologists are overwhelmed with patients at the moment but do not give up hope. Talk to your friends, your colleagues, your neighbours - someone will know someone and can hopefully get you in somewhere. For me here in Aotearoa New Zealand, I accessed counselling services through the Employee Assistance Programme (EAP Services Ltd) as the Ministry of Education has a contract for all of their workers (teachers included). It was a straightforward process in calling to make an appointment and all completely confidential. The school I was working with at the time would have been notified that someone had accessed the services but not made aware of who had accessed it, which I think is also great in terms of removing barriers and respecting people's privacy.

I was nervous about my first appointment though as I had accessed counselling once before in the past while I was at university. The counsellor I met with at that time struck me as tired, uninterested and just doing her job (who I now look back on and feel compassion for). But it also made me uncomfortable and much less willing to share my thoughts. I never went back.

This time round however, I lucked in with an absolutely amazing lady who I've now been seeing on and off since 2016. Nicola has been and continues to be a godsend in providing me with a safe and honest space to dissect and reflect on the progress that I've been making.

She doesn't sugar-coat things for me which has been extremely beneficial in helping me to cut through the crap and make positive changes for the better.

Her ability to remain impartial, use prompting questions to challenge my views on things and her genuine sense of care for my wellbeing has contributed to my confidence growth and being able to live the life I want to. I am beyond grateful for her support and thank my lucky stars every day that I was able to find the kind of help that I needed.

But at one point in time, counselling wasn't enough for me on its own. I always thought it would be but I got to the stage where simply talking to someone just wasn't working. The argument over the benefits of medication for treatment of depression and other mental illnesses is still something that I frequently debate in my mind. And I know that it's something that a lot of us don't consider lightly. Yet when you break your arm, you get a cast put on it. When you injure yourself in a car crash, the doctors give you morphine for the pain and we think nothing of it. But when we struggle with depression, because it's the brain and it's such a complex organism and it's a different type of pain, I feel like there is often a barrier to the willingness of people to provide or to seek medication. Why is that? Where does that mindset come from? Simply put, it means that I'm admitting that I have a problem and that I need help. As mentioned earlier, that is one of the single most confronting parts of this whole process in terms of my experience.

We as New Zealanders tend to have this "she'll be right" mentality so admitting that you need help because your brain isn't working the way that it should poses a barrier in itself.

When really seeking help for any kind of pain should be something that comes as second nature. We seek medication for physical pain - why shouldn't it be sought for mental pain?

Medication for a lot of people can offer just the solution for what they need at that moment. Depression is a chemical imbalance resulting in the neurons in the brain not functioning the way that they should. Medication can assist to rewire those neurons to fire more effectively. From what I've learnt over the past few years, serotonin is a drug that is released by the body/brain that makes us feel happy. When a person is experiencing feelings of depression over a long period of time, the serotonin being released is suppressed considerably, if it's released at all. Medication acts to rewire the neurotransmitters to send those messages to the brain that elicit feelings of happiness and being content - essentially stabilizing our mood, positively enhancing our wellbeing, our sleep and our eating patterns.

The effect that medication can have for a depressed person can make a world of difference if it is the right medication and the person has looked at and considered all the other options.

I'm not here to advocate for or against medication - I'm just here to tell you my story and my perspective so I need to make it really clear that I am not a doctor and have no qualifications in this area. This section is really about getting you to consider whether medication is right for you or for your loved one and to help you ask the necessary questions needed to make that decision.

For me, I resisted wanting to take medication for years. I felt that if I was to go down that track it would make everything more real. I had this preconceived notion that if I was on medication, it meant that something was wrong. Yes, I know I was dealing with mental illness but I thought I could manage it differently. For a time, I was able to do so. But then I found that things got on top of me when they shouldn't have. What I mean is that I was ticking along just fine - good family and friends, steady job, partner, sport, life was good.

And yet I was struggling. The cloud had reappeared and was casting its shadow over every aspect of my life.

I couldn't seem to kick it no matter what I tried. I was exercising as much as I could - keep in mind that when someone is depressed, energy levels are severely depleted and exercise (although highly beneficial) seemed like an insurmountable task. I was trying all my tools I mentioned earlier in terms of self-care but nothing was working.

So, I went to my GP. I hadn't been seeing her all that long as I had recently moved to Wellington. We discussed my situation in depth. She asked some questions that were primarily around my self-care tools and what I had been doing already to look after myself. The fact that none of these were working was a key indicator that something needed to change. Thankfully, she decided that medication was necessary and prescribed me some antidepressants. I didn't know a whole lot about the drugs but knew that it took a while for them to build up in my system and to notice the effects.

The first couple of variations my GP prescribed did not work for me. I really want to highlight this as it's important to trust your instincts and your body and to say something if you don't feel they're right for you. I had a few minor side effects and communicated this to my doctor. She changed me from the SSRI type (selective serotonin reuptake inhibitors) to an SNRI (selective norepinephrine reuptake inhibitors) and that made a massive difference for me. After a couple of months, I started to notice a difference in my mood and my ability to function more effectively on a daily basis.

I finally felt like myself and I was able to maintain a consistent approach to life.

My moods weren't as extreme anymore, I could focus on tasks for longer periods of time, I was sleeping better and my general demeanour improved. I enjoyed being myself again.

I remained on medication for a year. The first few months were really to allow it to kick in and then observe the effects over a longer period of time. I made the decision to stop taking the pills at the end of the teaching year and during summer after consulting with my GP. This was because I didn't have the additional pressures of work and there was the opportunity to be outside, soaking up the sun and taking part in general outdoor activities.

I felt confident enough in myself that I was able to cope on my own so I started tapering off.

I'm not going to lie - there were side effects while stopping that weren't that nice (headaches, drowsiness, nausea, dizziness) but they only lasted a couple of weeks. And then funnily enough, I felt like myself yet again. Looking back, the medication did exactly what I needed it to do. It gave me the chance to live my life more steadily and to get that sense of enjoyment back. Medication might not be right for your family member or friend but it is definitely an option to consider.

Exercise is the third and final strategy of what I like to refer to as the "triple threat" approach to depression. You can engage in medication, counselling and exercise in any way you choose - one at a time, a selection of two or a combination of all three. It's just about finding what works best for you.

Exercise or physical activity is something that when I was initially writing this section I had left out. I planned to just focus on medication and counselling. However, I'm a physical education teacher at heart, I have played sports and been active all throughout my life and the benefits I have experienced from being physically active extend beyond what I can truly measure.

As I mentioned earlier, when I have experienced a depressive episode my ability to exercise decreases substantially, if I can even bring myself to exercise at all. The funny thing about depression is that even though it is a mental illness, the impact on all four aspects of your wellbeing is considerable, especially with regards to how it can manifest physically. Sir Mason Durie's Te Whare Tapa Wha model uses the whare (house) as a representation of a person's hauora - their wellbeing. The whare has a foundation and a roof with four walls holding it up.

Each wall represents one aspect of our wellbeing - taha tinana (physical), taha hinengaro (mental and emotional), taha whānau (social) and taha wairua (spiritual). When one of these walls is impacted or is not cared for, the other walls suffer as well.

I truly love this model and what it represents for New Zealanders in terms of approaching our wellbeing. But for me, it really draws on how each aspect of our wellbeing can influence and impact the other aspects. My energy levels while in a depressive state are minimal to non-existent. The thought of going for a run around the block or a thirty-minute workout gives me extreme anxiety and the motivation to be physically active disappears in an instant. However, I know that being physically active can play such an important part in getting myself out of that state and therefore its importance as one of my key tools cannot be forgotten.

So, we start small.

What I have found is that just getting outside for a walk even if it is just for ten minutes gets those endorphins going and makes me feel slightly better. I've never got home and felt worse (yes, I will be tired of course but the fresh air and the movement brings progress). I also really enjoy walking along the beach and know that being close to the water is always a special place for me.

There's just something about the waves crashing into the shore, the salty air and the wind blowing (especially in Wellington) that enhances my wairua (my spirit) and picks me up again.

We're so lucky here in New Zealand to be surrounded by beautiful beaches and waterways - so I cannot recommend spending time outside enough. When the energy comes back to me and the depressive period is over, I find that regular physical activity is paramount in maintaining a positive mindset. I try to exercise 4-5 times a week and vary this between high intensity home workouts, longer runs at a medium pace, walks or hiking, indoor netball, touch rugby, snowboarding - the list goes on. I've never really been a gym person so instead I invested in some gear for at home as I believe it's about removing those barriers and I know that exercise is integral for me to be well. It's also about keeping that mindset as I always feel better after movement.

If your family member or friend is struggling with motivation to be physically active, a walk with a friend could help. Don't expect big things - a half marathon ain't going to happen anytime soon!

But pushing them to come for a small walk and to get some fresh air might not seem so scary.

It can also provide another opportunity to talk (or not). I've found that walking and talking is easier than just sitting and talking - as the focus is on the activity and not primarily on the person. Trying not to stereotype here but for some blokes, this could be just the key to help them open up. A walk with a mate also benefits the social aspect of our wellbeing as mentioned earlier - creating another connection to something positive in their life. Find something physical that they enjoy and offer to participate with them. Who knows - it might just benefit you as well!

Ah, kindness.
What a simple way to tell
another struggling soul that
there is love to be found in
the world.

9

Covid

Wowee - am I even allowed to say the word yet?! In my mind, that word has become the new "cancer" of our society. I think it's safe to say that the complete impacts of this pandemic are yet to be seen, as the world continues navigating its way through uncertainty, stress and disbelief. For someone living with depression, a pandemic could and probably has triggered a potentially devastating episode. I was lucky during the first lockdown... although the next paragraph may convince you otherwise. You be the judge.

I'd moved in with my partner at the time about a month before we went into New Zealand's first Level 4 lockdown.

Into a one-bedroom apartment.

In Wellington.

Facing south, with no green space.

I'd suggested to him that maybe we head up to the Coast for lockdown to my parents' place, thinking about a much bigger house with rooms and a lawn. Understandably, he said he'd rather stay in town so I thought, why not? I mean, I like my parents but they're not his; and we love each other, we've just moved in together and we're going to have all of this time together. What could go wrong? I moved out two weeks later.

I must highlight a memorable moment however, when a friend sent me a Snapchat video of her mimicking an emergency fire drill with her husband. I thought this was a wonderful idea as we were both teachers and we just wanted to keep our other halves safe. So, in true Katie spirit, I "sounded my siren" - as loud as I could and proceeded to try to evacuate the building. Unfortunately, my partner didn't find this quite as amusing as I did. Thus, I know I'm not completely faultless as to how things turned out. Now I know in level 4 there were serious restrictions in place so I made my decision to leave my partner carefully.

If I'd been honest with myself, I knew the issues had been brewing for a while and were just simmering under the surface.

I recognised my triggers (being particularly stressed out) and could feel the situation spiralling. By now I'd become quite adept at getting on top of things early but Covid was a whole new ball game. I mean, a global pandemic with words such as unprecedented, isolation, quarantine and social-distancing quickly becoming part of our everyday vocabulary along with Jacinda's daily 1pm updates as the highlight of our days - such a different and far-fetched version of reality.

The stress in itself was hard to deal with for a number of reasons but coupled with the uncertainty of not knowing when this was going to end... It was tough. Don't get me wrong - as a teacher, I basked in the freedom of exercising when I wanted to and if I was annoyed with a student, I had the ability to simply put them on mute. If only I could still do that now!!!

But I craved the human connection.

When you're used to mixing with up to 100 students per day plus all of your colleagues, not seeing them in person everyday takes a lot of adjustment. And I'll bet I'm not the only one who had similar feelings. Because of this, and I don't say it lightly - the many impacts of Covid on our mental health as humans is yet to be seen, and I'm concerned about the already struggling system and its inability to cope. New Zealand just doesn't have the professionals, the money or the scope to be able to address our mental health crisis and Covid will add an extra kilo or two to an already weighted baggage.

This is why I believe now is really the time to show our humanity to one another not only here in Aotearoa but all over the world.

The message to "be kind" cannot be said enough because our experiences through this pandemic are so varied that we really have no idea what it's been like and continues to be like for people.

For one young adult, they may be living alone and not working due to the lockdown restrictions but receiving the government subsidy. For another person, they might have lost their job while still needing to provide for their whānau of six and not know if they will be employable in future. For another person, lockdown may have meant that their partner now has no outlet for their anger so takes it out on them and the children. Domestic violence rates have increased during the pandemic and it is a sad but harsh reality for a lot of families.

Not being able to feed your whānau or to access healthcare.

Kiwis stuck overseas and unable to get home to see their loved ones.

Family members passing away and funerals being limited in numbers for attendance or for some, not being able to attend at all.

The list goes on so we can only begin to imagine the impacts that this will have on people in the years to come. The subsequent lockdowns and isolation periods will have all impacted on us differently so continuing to show kindness where possible (it is always possible) will benefit us all.

In some ways, I believe it will help us build resilience but we need to continue talking to each other. To show kindness and empathy - imagine walking a mile in someone else's shoes. Provide space for someone to share their experience with you. With empathy, kindness and understanding, we can actually help each other. Having conversations about our shared or different experiences unites us and ultimately leads us to not feeling so alone.

you were put on this earth
to achieve
your greatest self,
to live out your purpose,
and to
do it courageously.

10

Living life every day

Writing this book has allowed me to truly dig deep and reflect on some of my most vulnerable moments in the simple hope that it can help others. Our minds are so complex, our emotions are far-reaching and our mental health is ever present as a need to be a high priority. Yet the resourcing here in Aotearoa New Zealand is considerably lacking and the strain on the system keeps bulging at the seams. I can only emphasise and stress here that **prevention** is the key. The ambulance at the bottom of the hill DOES NOT suffice and will continue to do more harm than good as families resent not being able to access help sooner.

Prevention means educating our tamariki: that they can feel less pressure than the expectations that society places upon them; that they can experience a range of emotions and they can simply be kids. There is also the need to build resilience through knowing that it is okay to fail but that you don't give up trying.

Prevention means checking in on your loved ones regularly and reassuring them that even though they might not feel it at the moment, that things **will** be okay.

Prevention means asking the tough questions even if you don't have the answers because sometimes it may just be about not feeling so alone. That someone cares enough to be there.

We live in a world where sadly life is busy. People are busy. Time is of the essence. But we need to make time for our people. For our loved ones. We need to make time to have meaningful conversations but we also need to make time to laugh and be silly.

Do I think there is one right way to approach this? Not at all. But throughout this book, I have given examples of tips, questions, advice and support that has helped me along the way. I've also highlighted some of the things that I wish had been done and can hopefully assist others on their journey towards wellness.

I don't think that this journey will ever truly end for me as I believe that we have to work every day on our wellbeing. We have to put ourselves first and prioritise our love for ourselves above all else.

But our loved ones can make a difference. Friends and whānau have the power to reach out and show a person struggling with mental illness that all hope is not lost. We have the ability to support each other through the simplest of gestures - a cup of tea, a text message, a hug or a visit to sit and yarn. In a world that is heading towards relationships through a screen, it is vital now more than ever that we focus on the people in front of us. It is vital that we stop placing importance on the likes we get for a photo and rather place importance on the time we spend laughing and enjoying our loved ones' company. Because we can never get that time back.

Time is precious. And that time together really can fulfil our souls.

I'm in a much better place now but that's not to say I don't still have bad days. I'm just more aware now of how to deal with those days more effectively - speak with a friend, go for a run, listen to music, read inspiring/empowering quotes.

Mental illness is a daily reminder of how the brain functions and how it can turn you against yourself. It's an acknowledgement that when I wake up in the morning, I make a choice to focus on my wellbeing, and to put ME first. It's not selfish because I know that I have to work at it EVERY DAY to ensure that I have the best quality of life and that I get the most out of my days.

Sometimes that means I lie on the couch and watch tv. And that's okay. Other times it means I'll go for a run to clear my head, and to tick off that half marathon. Sometimes it means staying up late, writing a blog post to reflect on what I've been through and the person I am today. I guess I kinda like her.

Now that I've shared part of my story, I hope I can inspire others to share theirs. Let's all be brave and help one another. Let's break the stigma. Be kind, because everyone you meet is fighting their own battle.

It's okay to not be okay.

Coping strategies

These are some strategies that I used at different times to help me cope. You could suggest one of these (or a number of these) to help support your loved one.

Ask for Help

Reach out to family, friends or a counsellor.

Healthy Nutrition

Go back to basics and make simple meals with protein and vegetables.

Keep Your Mind Busy

Read a book, watch a movie or tv show or play a card/board game.

No Social Media

Log out of your accounts or delete the apps so the temptation for scrolling is gone.

Carry a Special Object

For me, it was a crystal. I would hold onto it when I was feeling anxious and a wave of calm would come over me and ground me.

Exercise

Go for a walk, a run, or a home workout such as boxing, yoga or stretching.

No Alcohol

Cut out the urge to go to the bottle and replace with soda water or water with lemon.

Head to the Beach

Sit by the water and just breathe.

Live in the Moment

Focus on your breath, and living for the day.

Little Treats

Reward yourself for doing the little things. Chocolate, a massage, buying something for yourself.

Self-Care

Wash your hair, paint your nails, do a face mask. Have a bubble bath.

Day Off

I would often feel guilty about this but it was so needed. Take a day off from work, from kids, from any responsibility. Just take a day.

Drink More Water

Add lemon or cucumber to freshen it up.

Enjoy the Little Things

Have a cup of tea or coffee, a phone call to a friend and have a good nights' sleep.

Chill Time

Light some candles and listen to your favourite playlist.

Positive Affirmations

Write yourself post-it notes with positive quotes or affirmations and put them around your room or the house.

Appreciate Yourself

A reminder in the morning that you're worth it.

Meditate

Take five minutes out of your day to just focus on your breathing. Close your eyes and be in the moment.

"Never underestimate the importance of your health and happiness, and never, ever apologise for putting yourself first."

"You are incredible. You make this world a little more wonderful. You have so much potential and so many things left to do. You have time. Better things are coming your way, so please hang in there. You can do it."

13 Reminders

1. The past is in the past – focus on the future.

2. Opinions do not define reality.

3. Everyone's journey is different.

4. Time is the essence of healing.

5. Judgement is a confession of character.

6. Overthinking will lead to paralysis/sadness.

7. Happiness is an inside job, found within.

8. Positive thoughts create positive actions.

9. Smiles are contagious.

10. Sprinkle kindness – it's free.

11. You only fail if you quit/do not try.

12. What goes around, comes around.

13. The quicker you choose to move forward, the quicker the suffering ends.

Acknowledgements

Writing this book has not only taught me patience but it has also shown me the amount of love I have in my life. I'm so grateful to everyone who has helped me on this journey - but a few special mentions:

To George Jahnke for inspiring me to start. All it takes is five lines a day. Here we are, a whole book later. Thank you for the push.

To Falstaff Mitchell for editing the original version chapter by chapter. You didn't know me from a bar of soap but took on the challenge anyway. I so appreciated your questions, your impartiality and your feedback along the way. The book wouldn't be where it's at without your help. Thank you.

To one of my longest and dearest friends, Vanessa Edridge - you are a star. Not only have you been a friend to me all these years but your graphic design finesse has shaped this book into what it is now. You listened to my suggestions and created the vision I had from the start, even if the technology sometimes didn't do what we wanted! I appreciate you more than you know. Thank you.

To my counsellor Nicola, where to even start. You were my rock throughout some of my toughest moments and always offered wise, practical and thoughtful suggestions. You helped me immensely and I'll forever be in debt to you for keeping me in line - people, find yourself a Nicola! Thank you, thank you.

To Jen, another godsend in the form of a second mother. You are family to me and have always provided consistent safety, wise words and staunch opinions. You know me better than I know myself and I'm blessed that you welcomed this little pale-skinned sister into your whānau. Love you muchly, Shorty x

To my Australian counterpart Tamara - from the moment we met I knew we were destined to be friends for life. You are always at the end of the phone, a message away or just a four hour flight! No matter the distance, you've got my back and I've got yours. Thank you for being you.

To the best friend a girl could ever ask for - Tara. We have grown together over the years like sisters; we have laughed, we have cried, we have loved but most of all we have persevered. You are a beautiful woman inside and out, and I couldn't be more proud of the person you are. Thank you for welcoming me into your family as well, and for the key to the bach. Love you.

Last, but definitely not least, to my family. Anna, you continue to inspire me with your positive outlook, your kindness and your warmth. I love you like a sister and am super proud of the beautiful human you are. Matt - thank you for looking out for me over the years, for the sand in the diapers and the laughs over a bevvie or three.

To my Abigail and Tommy - there is no other love like an Aunty's love. You taught me what it's like to love unconditionally and wholeheartedly. I love watching you grow and will always be proud of all that you achieve.

Mum and Dad - thank you for raising me to be this strong, independent and assertive woman. You've instilled values in me from a young age and I wouldn't be half the person I am without you. All the early morning netball games, the bank of Dad, the roof over my head and dinner on the table at night - I'm forever grateful. I know we've butted heads along the way Dad but I respect your drive, your ambition and your pragmatic approach to life. I love watching you be Grumps to Abigail and Tommy and seeing them light up when you and Nana arrive. They love you both so much. Mum, I'm beyond blessed that you chose me as your daughter. The kindness and warmth you always show in your quiet and unassuming manner doesn't go unnoticed and I'm lucky to have you as my Mum. Thank you both for being there for me and trying to understand as best as you could. It means a lot. I love you.

www.ingramcontent.com/pod-product-compliance
Lightning Source LLC
Chambersburg PA
CBHW060515280326
41933CB00014B/2970